ふるさとの名庭

A CELEBRATION OF JAPANESE GARDENS

日弁貞夫

写真集

「地方名庭園によせて」　吉河　功　　4

6　　The Regional Gardens of Japan　　Isao Yoshikawa

目　次
CONTENTS

桂離宮庭園　　10　　Katsura Imperial Villa Garden

仙洞御所庭園　　14　　Sentou Imperial Palace Garden

修学院離宮庭園　　18　　Shuugakuin Imperial Villa Garden

玉川寺庭園　　22　　Gyokusen-ji Temple Garden

白水阿弥陀堂庭園　　23　　Shiramizu Amida-do Garden

偕楽園　　24　　Kairakuen Garden

輪王寺逍遥園　　26　　Shouyouen Garden, Rinnou-ji Temple

清澄庭園　　28　　Kiyozumi Garden

皇居東御苑二の丸庭園　　32　　Ninomaru Garden, East Garden of the Imperial Palace

旧芝離宮庭園　　34　　Former Shiba Imperial Villa Garden

三渓園　　36　　Sankeien Garden

清水園　　38　　Shimizuen Garden

玉泉　　40　　Gyokusenen Garden

下時国家庭園　　42　　Shimotokikuni Family Garden

柴田氏庭園　　44　　Shibata Residence Garden

旧玄成院庭園　　46　　Former Genjo-in Temple Garden

朝倉氏諏訪館跡庭園　　48　　Ruins of Suwa-yakata, Asakura Residence Garden

円照寺庭園　　49　　Ensho-ji Temple Garden

龍潭寺庭園　　50　　Ryutan-ji Temple Garden

摩訶耶寺庭園　　51　　Makaya-ji Temple Garden

妙厳寺庭園　　52　　Myogon-ji Temple Garden

地蔵院庭園　　54　　Jizo-in Temple Garden

諸戸氏庭園　　56　　Moroto Family Garden

西明寺庭園　　58　　Saimyouji Temple Garden

金剛輪寺庭園　　60　　Kongourin-ji Temple Garden

多賀神社奥書院庭園　　62　　Taga-jinja Shrine, Oku-shoin Garden

大通寺庭園　　63　　Daitsu-ji Temple, Ganzanken Garden

普門院庭園	64	Fumon-in Temple Garden
天徳院庭園	66	Tentoku-in Temple Garden
和歌山城紅葉渓庭園	68	Momiji-dani Garden, Wakayama Castle
南禅寺金地院庭園	70	Nanzen-ji Temple, Konchi-in Garden
本法寺庭園	71	Hompou-ji Temple Garden
大徳寺瑞峰院庭園	72	Daitoku-ji Temple, Zuiho-in Garden
大徳寺竜源院庭園	73	Daitoku-ji Temple, Ryogen-in Garden
城南宮楽水園	74	Jounan-gu Rakusuien Garden
勧持院庭園	75	Kanji-in Temple Garden
普門寺庭園	76	Fumon-ji Temple Garden
安養院庭園	78	Anyou-in Temple Garden
深田氏庭園	80	Fukuda Residence Garden
興禅寺庭園	81	Kouzen-ji Temple Garden
衆楽園	82	Jurakuen Garden
桂氏邸庭園	84	Katsura Residence Garden
毛利家本邸庭園	86	Mouri Central Residence Garden
万象園	87	Banshouen Garden
西江寺庭園	88	Seigou-ji Temple Garden
光明寺庭園	89	Koumyou-ji Temple Garden
水前寺成趣園	90	Suizenji, Joushuen Garden
仙巌園（磯庭園）	92	Senganen (Iso) Garden
庭園解説　吉河　功	93	Explanation of Gardens　Isao Yoshikawa
「庭園様式について」　吉河　功	102	
	104	The Styles of Japanese Gardens　Isao Yoshikawa
	105	
あとがき	106	Postscript

ブックデザイン：奥山有美
BOOK DESIGN　YUMI OKUYAMA

「地方名園によせて」

吉河 功
日本庭園研究家

4

日本庭園というと，大抵の人は京都こそがその本場だと思っている。

たしかに，各時代の名園を，まとめて手軽に観賞出来る土地といえば，京をおいて他にないであろう。

「京都の庭は美しい」と誰もがいう。それも間違いのない事実である。日本を代表する観光地でもあり，庭師の水準も高いから，ほとんどの庭は立派に手入れがなされており，きれいで親しみやすい。

しかし，一面において京都は平安朝以来の都であり，大都市であったから，応仁ノ乱のような戦乱や，火災も多く，それだけに庭園にも変化が多かった。一部の名園を除いては，作庭当初のままに残っている庭は案外少ない。表面的には美しくても，保存率はそれ程ではなく，改修された美ともいえる。

庭園に少し深い趣味を持っている人に聞くと，「地方に名園が多いことに感心する」という人が多い。これには筆者も同感である。

日本を代表する極めつきの名園を上げて行くと，意外にも地方の庭園の方が，京都の庭よりはるかに数が多いことに気付かされる。

かつての都といっても，一地域と，日本全国とを比較したのでは，全国の方がはるかに庭の数が多いのは当然の結果なのである。

地方の庭園は，総対的にいって手入れの不十分なものが多く，また土に埋もれて発掘の必要がある庭さえある。それだけに，一見すると粗野な感じを受けやすい。

しかし，そのために，かえって当初の造形がよく保存されている例も多く，いわば“磨けば光る庭”なのである。

さらにそれらの庭園は，京の「みやび」に対して，地方武士的な「素朴な力強さ」にあふれている。いわば“純な魂のある庭”ということができよう。

日本庭園を代表する豪華な石組の庭などは，地方に例が多く，地方名園の一特色といってもよい程である。

全国的に見ると，地方文化が発達した土地には，必ず名園が多く作庭されている。

京都の周辺でも，滋賀県や兵庫県には名園が多いし，北陸地方の福井県，中部地方

の山梨県や長野県にも庭園の数が多い。

　古く平安時代には，今の岩手県平泉に奥州藤原氏三代の文化が開け，多くの庭園が作られたこともよく知られている。

　近世では，京より江戸に都が移ったため，現在の東京の地に多数の庭園が作られていた事実もあるが，残念ながら後に大部分が失われてしまった。

　また，名石が豊富にある地方に庭園が発達したことも忘れてはならない。青石の名石「阿波石」の産地である徳島県などはその好例といえよう。

　さらに各地には，それぞれ文化性の違いがあるから，そこに作られる庭園にも地方色にあふれた独特の造形感覚があり，それを理解することも一つの楽しみである。

　桃山時代以降では，城郭庭園，大名庭園といった，京都にはあまり例のない作庭が多いことも地方ならではといえよう。

　本書には，京都の名園の他に，これら地方の隠れた名園も多く紹介されている。

　その中には，朝倉氏諏訪館跡庭園(福井市)のような巨石による豪華極まりない作から，石組の味わい深さと，構成力の確かさでは全国屈指の摩訶耶寺庭園(静岡県)，あるいは城郭庭園の代表作である和歌山城紅葉渓庭園(和歌山市)，中国式の風景を意図した大通寺庭園(長浜市)などがあり，なかなか変化に富んでいる。

　全国にちらばっているこれらの名園を実際に観賞するのは容易ではないが，本書によってしばし名園の旅をしてみるのも，また一興というものであろう。

　ただし，庭園というものは，写真だけではどうしても一面的な美しさしか表現できにくいという宿命を持っている。

　それは庭園が立体的な，奥行きを重視した造形であるからにほかならない。

　特に石組を主体とした名園程，その美を表現するのは難しいものである。

　多方面からの観賞を意図している庭園を，どの方面から捉えるか，ということも重要な問題となる。この場合は，庭園に対する理解度が特に要求されるのである。

　さらに季節や天候，また時刻によってさえも庭園の表情は大きく変化する。

　手入れの不十分な庭も困りものである。これらのすべてを克服して，納得する写真を撮るには，何度も現地へ足を運ばなくてはならない。そういう苦労の結晶として，写真集は完成するものであって，本書も撮影者の感性がよく出た作品といえると思う。

　そして，本書を参考として，気に入った庭園があったならば，ぜひ多くの皆様に実際の庭園を観賞していただきたいというのが，筆者の切なる願いである。

The Regional Gardens of Japan

Isao Yoshikawa
Garden Researcher

6

Most people would consider Kyoto to be the home of the Japanese garden, and it is probably true that there is no place except the old capital where one can easily see examples of great gardens from every age. Everyone agrees that Kyoto's gardens are lovely. There is no mistake. Kyoto is the garden capital of Japan. The standards of craftsmanship are so high that virtually all the gardens exhibit splendid elements, are beautiful and even easy to fall in love with.

Kyoto was the capital of Japan from the Heian period, and therefore its greatest city, and suffered through the Onin Wars, and the ravages of fire, so it is no surprise there is such variation in its garden styles. In fact, with the exception of a few very famous gardens, all but a few have been altered from their original shapes. They are all still beautiful, but it is not because they have been perfectly preserved.

Actually, in talking to people who know gardens well one often hears it said: "In the country one find more great gardens." The author of this book would agree.

In fact, in discussing the famous gardens of Japan one comes to realize that the far greater number of these are not found in Kyoto, but in the outlying areas of the country. Naturally, it is not surprising that there are more fine examples of gardens throughout the rest of the country than in the one one-time capital.

But in the countryside many of the great gardens have not been well cared for, and a few remain to be fully unearthed from the ground. Just one look sometimes gives the impression of a very overrun quality. But for the same reason the original shape of these gardens is often quite well preserved, and can be brought out beautifully with a little polishing.

Moreover, as opposed to the elegance of the capital's gardens, the country gardens have more of the force of the country samurai, and can perhaps even be said to be "gardens of pure spirit."

Many of the most beautiful garden rock formations are to be found in the gardens of the country.

If one looks at a map of the entire country, it becomes

clear that the cultural centers of the land are also the places where great gardens are found.

Near Kyoto, one finds great gardens in Shiga and Hyogo prefectures, and there are also great gardens in Fukui, on the Japan Sea aide, and in Yamanashi and Nagano prefectures, in central Honshu.

During the ancient Heian period, around Hiraizumi in Iwate prefecture, the cultural flourishing of the third lord Oushu Fujiwara gave rise to the construction of many gardens.

In more recent times the capital was moved to Edo, and during this period many gardens were built as well. Unfortunately, most of the gardens of Edo have been lost.

Also, the best stones for garden landscaping are found in the country, with a fine example being that of the *awaishi* bluestone, which is quarried in Tokushima prefecture.

Furthermore, one finds in the gardens of the country elements of local culture which make them unique; coming to understand the local flavorings is another pleasure of garden-viewing.

After the Momoyama period much of the garden building was done at castle residences and the homes of the *daimyo*, and here again one sees garden styles which are not found in Kyoto.

In this book, besides some famous gardens of Kyoto, a great number of hidden treasures from the country are introduced.

Among these are the Asakura Residence Suwayakata Garden Ruins (Fukui Prefecture), with its inexpressably beautiful colossal stone, and the Makaya-ji Temple Garden (Shizuoka prefecture), with its brilliant rock formations and unsurpassed layout, or, among castle residence gardens, the Momiji-dani Garden of Wakayama Castle (Wakayama), or again, in the Chinese style, the garden Daitsuji (Nagahama). The styles are extremely varied.

It is certainly not easy to view all of these famous gardens, which are spread from one end of the country to the other, but by studying this book one is taking something of an excursion through the famous gardens of the country. This is not to say that photos can capture the full beauty of the gardens; that, perhaps, is the fate of all photographs. In any case, the garden is above all a creation of depth and physical form, making it impossible for anything but the human eye to fully appreciate. The rock formations are perhaps the hardest aspect of the garden to grasp from a photograph. Japanese gardens are constructed to be viewed from various positions, and positioning itself becomes a very delicate problem. Naturally, season and time of day also have a great bearing upon the appearance of the garden.

Moreover, there are gardens which simply lack enough prominent features. In order to overcome all of these problems, and produce photographs that satisfy the eye, it has been necessary to return to locations many times to retake pictures. The result of these efforts is this book, and the quality of the pictures it contains attests to the dedication of the photographer.

Finally, it is the hope of the author that readers will find among these landscapes one which is particularly to their liking, and that the book will encourage many people to visit and see for themselves the beauty of Japanese gardens.

A CELEBRATION OF JAPANESE GARDENS

Photographs by Sadao Hibi ©
Translations by Scott Brause

First Edition March 1994
ISBN4-7661-0744-6

Graphic-sha Publishing Company Ltd.
1-9-12 Kudan-kita Chiyoda-ku Tokyo 102 Japan
Phone 03-3263-4318
Fax 03-3263-5297

Printed in Japan by Nissha Printing Co., Ltd.

A CELEBRATION OF JAPANESE GARDENS

Photographs by SADAO HIBI

10

1　桂離宮庭園　　新書院とサツキ　江戸時代初期・京都市西京区
Katsura Imperial Villa Garden. The *shin-shoin* (new drawing room) and sculpted azaleas. Early Edo period, Nishigyo-ku, Kyoto.

2 桂離宮庭園　　天の橋立付近と松琴亭　江戸時代初期・京都市西京区
The stone bridge and *Shoukintei*, Katsura Imperial Villa Garden. Early Edo period, Nishigyo-ku, Kyoto.

12

3　桂離宮庭園　　書院の月見台と池泉　江戸時代初期・京都市西京区
The drawing room's moon-viewing porch and pond, Katsura Imperial Villa Garden. Early Edo period, Nishigyo-ku, Kyoto.

4　桂離宮庭園　　古書院御輿寄前庭の織部灯籠と庭門　江戸時代初期・京都市西京区
Oribe stone garden lantern and gate, front garden, Katsura Imperial Villa Garden. Early Edo period, Nishigyo-ku, Kyoto.

14

5　仙洞御所庭園　　石浜より醒花亭を望む　江戸時代初期・京都市上京区
Sentou Imperial Palace Garden. The *Suikatei* as seen from the stone beach. Early Edo period, Kamigyo-ku, Kyoto.

16

6 仙洞御所庭園　　池畔の芝浜と園路　江戸時代初期・京都市上京区
The garden path along the grass beach on the hillock (*chihan*), Sentou Imperial Palace Garden. Early Edo period, Kamigyo-ku, Kyoto.

18

7　修学院離宮庭園　　上の御茶屋・隣雲亭からの展望　江戸時代初期・京都市左京区
Kaminoochaya, Shuugakuin Imperial Villa Garden. The view from *Rin'untei*. Early Edo period, Sakyo-ku, Kyoto.

20

9　修学院離宮庭園　　上の御茶屋の船屋から見る浴竜池　江戸時代初期・京都市左京区
Shuugakuin Imperial Villa Garden. Yokuryu pond viewed from Kaminoochaya. Early Edo period, Sakyo-ku, Kyoto.

22

10　玉川寺庭園　　池泉左手からの全景　江戸時代初期・山形県東田川郡
Gyokusen ji Temple Garden. A full view of the garden as seen from the left side. Early Edo period, Higashitagawa gun, Yamagata Prefecture.

23

11　白水阿弥陀堂庭園　　園池を通して阿弥陀堂(国宝) を見る　平安時代・福島県いわき市
Shiramizu Amida-do Garden. The *Amida-do* (national treasure) as seen from across the pond. Iwaki, Fukushima Prefecture.

24

12 偕楽園　　紅梅を通して好文亭を望む　江戸時代末期・茨城県水戸市
Kairakuen. *Koubuntei* and a blossoming plum tree. Late Edo period, Mito, Ibaragi Prefecture.

13 偕楽園　　朝霧の偕楽園・松と竹垣　江戸時代末期・茨城県水戸市
Kairakuen. A pine tree and bamboo fence in morning mist. Late Edo period, Mito, Ibaragi Prefecture.

14 輪王寺逍遥園　中島と塔灯籠　江戸時代初期・栃木県日光市
Shouyouen Garden, Rinnou-ji Temple. Central island and stone lantern. Early Edo period, Nikko, Tochigi Prefecture.

15　輪王寺逍遥園　　亭と建仁寺垣　江戸時代末期・栃木県日光市
Dining hall and Kennin-ji bamboo fence, Shouyouen, Rinnou-ji Temple. Late Edo period, Nikko, Tochigi Prefecture.

16 清澄庭園　大飛石の園路　明治時代・東京都江東区
Kiyozumi Garden. The large stepping stone path. Meiji era, Koto-ku, Tokyo.

30

17　清澄庭園　　仙台石の大石橋　　明治時代・東京都江東区
Kiyomizu Garden. The bridge of large *Sendai* stone. Meiji era, Koto-ku, Tokyo

18　清澄庭園　　青石の沢渡石　明治時代・東京都江東区
Stepping stones of blue whetstone. Kiyomizu Garden. Meiji era, Koto-ku, Tokyo.

32

19　皇居東御苑二の丸庭園　　諏訪の茶屋の敷石　現代・東京都千代田区
East Garden of the Imperial Palace. Flagstone path by Suwa Teahouse, Ninomaru Garden, Modern period, Chiyoda-ku, Tokyo.

33

20　皇居東御苑二の丸庭園　菖蒲園　現代・東京都千代田区
Irises in Ninomaru Garden, East Garden of the Imperial Palace. Modern period, Chiyoda-ku, Tokyo.

34

21　旧芝離宮庭園　　潮入式の干潟と雪見灯籠　江戸時代初期・東京都港区
Former Shiba Imperial Villa garden Tidal flat and *yukimi* stone lantern. Early Edo period, Minato-ku, Tokyo.

22　旧芝離宮庭園　　西湖堤と蓬莱島　江戸時代初期・東京都港区
Former Shiba Imperial Villa garden. *Seiko-zutsumi* (the embankment of Lake Hsi Hu) and *horai* island. Early Edo period, Minato-ku, Tokyo.

36

23 三渓園　　池泉と板橋　　大正時代・神奈川県横浜市
The pond and wooden bridge in Sankeien Garden Taisho era, Yokohama, Kanagawa Prefecture.

24 三渓園　篠竹のある園路　大正時代・神奈川県横浜市
Sankeien Garden. The path through *shinotake* bamboo. Taisho era, Yokohama, Kanagawa Prefecture.

38

25 清水園　東部池畔の夕佳亭　江戸時代初期・新潟県新発田市
Shimizuen Garden. The *Sekkatei* on the east shore of the pond. Early Edo period, Shibata, Niigata Prefecture.

26　清水園　　池を渡る御影石の橋　江戸時代初期・新潟県新発田市
Granite bridge over the pond, Shimizuen Garden. Early Edo period, Shibata, Niigata Prefecture.

40

27 玉泉園　池泉岩島と雪見灯籠　江戸時代初期・石川県金沢市
Gyokusenen Garden. Rock island pond and *yukimi* stone lantern. Early Edo period, Kanazaw, Ishikawa Prefecture.

28 玉泉園　ススキと蒲の彫刻のある手水鉢　江戸時代初期・石川県金沢市
The water basin with miscanthus and cattail relief, Gyokusenen Garden. Early Edo period, Kanazawa, Ishikawa Prefecture.

29　下時国家庭園　　池泉岩島とサツキの刈り込み　江戸時代初期・石川県輪島市
Rock island pond and sculpted azaleas, Shimotokikuni Family Garden. Early Edo period, Wajima, Ishikawa Prefecture.

44

30　柴田氏庭園　　甘棠館の土橋と書院前の石浜　江戸時代初期・福井県敦賀市
Shibata Residence Garden. Pond and earthen bridge near the drawing room. Early Edo period, Tsuruga, Fukui Prefecture.

31 柴田氏庭園　　石浜より中島を望む　江戸時代初期・福井県敦賀市
Shibata Residence Garden. The central island viewed from the stone beach. Early Edo period, Tsuruga, Fukui Prefecture.

32　旧玄成院庭園　　杉林と築山　室町時代・福井県勝山市
Former Genjo-in Temple Garden. Cedars by the mound. Muromachi period, Katsuyama, Fukui Prefecture.

48

33 朝倉氏諏訪館跡庭園　　滝の巨大立石付近　桃山時代・福井県足羽郡
Ruins of Suwa-yakata at the Asakura Residence, near the waterfall and great standing rock. Momoyama period, Asuwa-gun, Fukui Prefecture.

34　円照寺庭園　　池泉中央部と山畔滝石組(左)　　江戸時代初期・福井県小浜市
Ensho-ji Temple Garden. The central pond, with the waterfall rock formation (left) and berm. Early Edo period, Obama, Fukui Prefecture.

50

35　龍潭寺庭園　築山枯滝付近の景　江戸時代初期・静岡県引佐郡
Ryutan-ji Temple Garden. Scenery near the mound and dry waterfall. Early Edo period, Inasa-gun, Shizuoka Prefecture.

36 摩訶耶寺庭園　　池畔石組より鶴島を望む　鎌倉時代・静岡県引佐郡
Makaya-ji Temple Garden. The crane island as seen from the shore rockery. Kamakura period, Inasa-gun, Shizuoka Prefecture.

37　妙厳寺庭園　　ソテツと塔灯籠　江戸時代初期・愛知県豊川市
Myougon-ji Temple Garden. Palms and stone lantern. Early Edo period, Toyokawa, Aichi Prefecture.

38　地蔵院庭園　　池泉に張り出した茶室の景　江戸時代中期・三重県鈴鹿郡
Jizo-In Temple Garden. Scenery around the teahouse. Middle Edo period, Suzuka-gun, Mie Prefecture.

39 　地蔵院庭園　　茶室丸窓より池畔のハギを見る　江戸時代中期・三重県鈴鹿郡
Jizo-in Temple Garden. Bush clover at the pond's edge, as seen through the teahouse window. Middle Edo period, Suzuka-gun, Mie Prefecture.

56

40 諸戸氏庭園　　礼拝石より池泉岩島を望む　明治時代・三重県桑名市
Moroto Family Garden. The rock island as seen from the prayer rock. Meiji era, Kuwana, Mie Prefecture.

57

41 諸戸氏庭園　　園路の敷石と藤棚　明治時代・三重県桑名市
Moroto Family Garden. The flagstone path under wisteria. Meiji era, Kuwana, Mie Prefecture.

58

42 西明寺庭園　　飛石道と池泉の半景　江戸時代中期・滋賀県犬上郡
Saimyou-ji Temple Garden. A partial view of the stepping stones and pond. Middle Edo period, Inukami-gun, Shiga Prefecture.

59

43 西明寺庭園　　池泉岩島より見る築山　　江戸時代中期・滋賀県犬上郡
Saimyou-ji Temple Garden. The rockery as seen from the rock island. Middle Edo period, Inukami-gun, Shiga Prefecture.

44 金剛輪寺庭園　　池泉舟石より滝石組を望む　江戸時代中期・滋賀県愛知郡
Kongourin-ji Temple Garden. The rock waterfall as seen from the boot stone in the pond. Middle Edo Period, Echi-gun, Shiga Prefecture.

45　金剛輪寺庭園　　中央石橋と宝篋印塔の景　江戸時代中期・滋賀県愛知郡
Kongourin-ji Temple Garden. A view of the central stone bridge and *houkyouin-tou*. Middle Edo period, Echi-gun, Shiga Prefecture.

46　多賀神社奥書院庭園　　東部出島付近と枝垂れ桜　桃山時代・滋賀県犬上郡
Taga-jinja Shrine, Oku-shoin Garden. The peninsula formation and weeping cherry by the east drawing room. Momoyama period, Inukami-gun, Shiga Prefecture.

63

47　大通寺含山軒庭園　　枯山水中島より枯滝を見る　江戸時代中期・滋賀県長浜市
Daitsu-ji Temple Ganzanken Garden. The *karetaki* as seen from the central rock island of the *karesansui*. Middle Edo period, Nagahama, Shiga Prefecture.

48 普門院庭園　　山畔利用の池泉庭園全景　江戸時代初期・和歌山県伊都郡
Fumon-in Temple Garden　A full view of the pond and *sampan* (hillock) garden. Early Edo period, Ito-gun, Wakayama Prefecture.

49　天徳院庭園　　池泉中央部の中島と岩島　江戸時代初期・和歌山県伊都郡
Tentoku in Temple Garden. Central island and rock island of the pond. Early Edo period, Ito-gun, Wakayama Prefecture.

50　和歌山城紅葉渓庭園　　敷石中に打たれた飛石園路　桃山時代・和歌山市
Momiji-dani Garden, Wakayama Castle. Central stepping stone path within paving stones. Momoyama period,
Wakayama.

51　和歌山城紅葉渓庭園　池泉青石護岸と板橋　桃山時代・和歌山市
Momiji-dani Garden, Wakayama Castle. Bluestone rockery by the pond with wooden bridge in background. Early Edo period, Wakayama.

52　南禅寺金地院庭園　　飛石から礼拝石を望む　江戸時代初期・京都市左京区
Nanzen-ji Temple, Konchi-in Garden. The worship stone as seen from the stepping stone path. Early Edo period, Sakyo-ku, Kyoto.

53　本法寺庭園　　幡をかたどった蓮池　桃山時代・京都市上京区
Hompou-ji Temple Garden's curiously-built lotus pond. Momoyama period, Kamigyo-ku, Kyoto.

54　大徳寺瑞峰院庭園　　北庭の十字をかたどった石組　現代・京都市北区
Daitoku-ji Temple, Zuiho in Garden　The cross-like rock formation in the north garden. Modern, Kita-ku, Kyoto.

73

55　大徳寺竜源院庭園　　北庭の枯山水の中心石組　室町時代・京都市北区
Daitoku-ji Temple, Ryogen-in Garden. The central rock formation of the north garden *karesansui*. Muromachi period, Kita-ku, Kyoto.

74

56　城南宮楽水苑　　園路ぎわの枝垂れ桜　現代・京都市伏見区
Jounangu Rakusuien Garden. The weeping cherries by the path. Modern, Fushimi-ku, Kyoto.

57 勧持院庭園　出島と石橋付近　桃山時代・京都市下京区
Kanji-in Temple Garden. Near the *dejima* and stone bridge. Momoyama period. Shimogyo-ku, Kyoto.

58　普門寺庭園　　横石主体の枯池式枯山水　江戸時代初期・大阪府高槻市
Fumon-Ji Temple Garden. The horizontal stone formation of the *kareike*-style *karesansui*. Early Edo period, Takatsuki, Osaka.

59　安養院庭園　　築山の亀石組を見る　桃山時代・兵庫県神戸市
Anyou-in Temple Garden. Looking towards the mound and turtle formation (*kameishi-gumi*). Momoyama period, Kobe.

60　安養院庭園　　仏手石の手水鉢　桃山時代・兵庫県神戸市
The Hand of Buddha stone water basin, Anyou-in Temple Garden. Momoyama period, Kobe, Hyogo Prefecture.

61 安養院庭園　　主石三尊と石橋付近　桃山時代・兵庫県神戸市
Near the three great rocks and stone bridge, Anyou-in Temple Garden. Momoyama period, Kobe, Hyogo Prefecture.

80

62 深田氏邸庭園　　池泉の鶴島(右)と亀島(左)　伝鎌倉時代・鳥取県米子市
Fukuda Residence Garden. Pond with crane island (right) and turtle (left). Kamakura period legend, Yonago, Tottori Prefecture.

63　興禅寺庭園　　出島と築山石組　江戸時代初期・鳥取市
Kouzen-ji Temple Garden. The *dejima* and mound formation. Early Edo period, Tottori.

82

64　衆楽園　　土橋より池畔の風月軒を見る　　江戸時代初期・岡山県津山市
Jurakuen Garden. *Fuugetsuken* and earthen bridge as viewed from the shore of the pond. Early Edo period, Tsuyama, Okayama Prefecture.

65 衆楽園　　芝浜落花の景　岡山県津山市
Fallen leaves on the *shibahama* (grass beach), Jurakuen Garden. Tsuyama, Okayama Prefecture.

84

66　桂氏邸庭園　　創作的な舟石の景　江戸時代末期・山口県防府市
Katsura Residence Garden. Creative *funaishi* (boat rock) scenery. Late Edo period, Bofu, Yamaguchi Prefecture.

85

67　桂氏邸庭園　　中央の伏石・横石・立石の主景石組　江戸時代末期・山口県防府市
The central "hidden", "flat" and "standing" stones, Katsura Residence Garden. Late Edo period, Bofu,
Yamaguchi Prefecture.

86

68　毛利家本邸庭園　　回遊路の石橋を望む　明治時代・山口県防府市
Mouri Central Residence Garden. A view of the bridge along the winding path. Meiji era, Bofu, Yamaguchi Prefecture.

69 万象園　平庭飛石より見る池畔の亭　江戸時代初期・香川県丸亀市
Banshouen Garden. The resthouse as seen from the stepping stones at the garden's edge. Early Edo period, Marugame, Kagawa Prefecture.

88

70 　西江寺庭園　　枯山水の飛石と石橋　江戸時代初期・愛媛県宇和島市
　　　Seigou-ji Temple Garden. The stepping stones and stone bridge of the *karesansui*. Early Edo period, Uwajima, Ehime Prefecture.

71 光明寺庭園　洲浜形の石浜と苔模様のある枯山水　現代・福岡県太宰府市
Koumyou-ji Temple Garden. The sandy beach-style stone beach and mossy *karesansui*. Modern, Dazaifu, Fukuoka Prefecture.

90

72 水前寺成趣園　清らかな湧き水池泉と芝山　江戸時代初期・熊本市
Suizenji, Joushuen Garden. The spring-fed pond and grassy hillock. Early Edo period, Kumamoto.

91

73　水前寺成趣園　　出島を通して古今伝授書院を望む　江戸時代初期・熊本市
Kokin-denju drawing room as seen past the *dejima*. Suizenji, Joushuen Garden. Early Edo period, Kumamoto.

92

74 仙巌園 (磯庭園)　　園内より見た借景の桜島　鹿児島市
Senganen Garden (Iso Garden). The view of Sakurajima from within the garden. Kagoshima.

庭園解説
EXPLANATION OF GARDENS

吉河　功
ISAO YOSHIKAWA

桂離宮庭園 　　　　　　　P10-13
江戸初期・京都市西京区

元和六年(1620)より八条宮家初代の智仁親王によって造営に着手された桂山荘。建築と庭園の多くは二代智忠親王の正保三年(1646)までに完成した。大規模な池泉回遊式庭園だが、基本的には当時の茶趣味から広大な露地の形式を持ち、敷石・飛石・石燈籠・手水鉢を配する。

白水阿弥陀堂庭園 　　　　　　P23
平安時代・福島県いわき市

平安時代後期の浄土庭園の様式を見せたもので、願成寺の園池。当寺は永暦元年(1160)頃、岩城則道の創立で、その室は藤原秀衡の妹徳姫であった。近年発掘整備された園池は、北にある阿弥陀堂を中心としたもので、東の池には当代の優れた感覚の岩島が保存されている。

皇居東御苑庭園 　　　　　　P32-33
江戸初期・東京都千代田区

旧江戸城の二の丸御殿に面して作庭された庭園で、寛永7年(1630)頃に着手、その後正保2年(1645)に改築された記録がある。今の庭は改造も多いが、池泉回遊式の庭園となり、美しく水を落とす滝石組を中心に、石浜や雪見燈籠を見せた豊かな景を見せている。

仙洞御所庭園 　　　　　　P14-17
江戸初期・京都市上京区

後水尾上皇の仙洞として寛永4年(1627)より、北にあった女院御所と共に着手され、初期の作庭には小堀遠州が関係している。江戸中期に女院御所との境がなくなり両者の池が合体した。南池にある広い石浜は、大きさのそろった石を用い、小田原一升石の浜といわれている。

偕楽園庭園 　　　　　　P24-25
江戸末期・茨城県戸市

水戸徳川家九代の徳川斉昭が営んだ梅園が初めで、天保12年(1840)頃には規模の大きな庭園とし、大衆と共に楽しむという意から「偕楽園」と命名した。園の中心には二層の「好文亭」を建て、千波湖の景色を眺める風情が重視されている。明治になって常磐公園とされた。

旧芝離宮庭園 　　　　　　P34-35
江戸初期・東京都港区

下総佐倉藩主大久保忠朝によって、延宝6年(1678)より作庭されたもので、「楽寿園」と命名されていた。元禄9年(1696)より東方に拡張され今日の姿となった。海水を取り入れた汐入式庭園の代表作で、広い園池に中島を浮かべ、そこに中国式の西湖堤を設けている。

94

修学院離宮庭園 　　　　　　P18-21
江戸初期・京都市左京区

後水尾上皇の離宮として明暦2年(1656)から造営にかかり、萬治2年(1659)に完成した。当初は「上の御茶屋」「下の御茶屋」から成り、前者の大規模な池泉と「隣雲亭」からの眺めがすばらしい。「中の御茶屋」は旧林丘寺で、明治になってから離宮に編入された。

輪王寺逍遙園 　　　　　　P26-27
江戸末期・栃木県日光市

東照宮の別当寺・天台宗の輪王寺庭園で、慶安元年(1648)直後の作庭と考えられる。男体山を望む地にあり、東西に長い池泉を掘り、東を流れ形式とした池泉回遊式の大庭園である。改造もあるが中島石組等には古い造形を保存し、特に五重の塔燈籠は江戸初期の名品である。

三渓園庭園 　　　　　　P36-37
大正時代・神奈川県横浜市

明治32年(1899)財閥原富太郎の山荘として着手され、明治41年頃に完成した池泉回遊式の大庭園。現在は内園と外園に分かれるが、特に内園には全国より優れた古建築や石造美術の名品を集めているのが特色。中心となる「臨春閣」付近のたたずまいはことに風雅である。

玉川寺庭園 　　　　　　P22
江戸初期・山形県東田川郡

羽黒町にある曹洞宗の古刹で、鎌倉中期の開創という。庭は書院北庭としての池泉観賞式庭園で、低い山畔に滝石組を設けて落水の景を見せ、三島の中島を作る。手前の飛石は明治時代の改修と思われる。石組感覚に優れるが、石が植栽で隠されているのは惜しい。

清澄園庭園 　　　　　　P28-31
明治時代・東京都江東区

江戸中期の大名・久世大和守の屋敷跡に、明治11年(1878)三井財閥の創始者岩崎弥太郎が作庭の工を起こしたもので、明治24年の完成。当時は隅田川から水を引いた汐入式庭園であった。広い園池に複数の中島を配し、全国各地より集めた名石で石組を行った豪華な作である。

清水園庭園 　　　　　　P38-39
江戸初期・新潟県新発田市

新発田藩主溝口氏三代の宣直の時、寛文6年(1665)頃当地に下屋敷清水谷御殿を完成し、この寛文年間に遠州流の茶人県宗智によって作庭されたという。広い池泉回遊式で、各所に書院・茶席を配した大名庭園の好例である。近年改修され、美しい姿を見せるようになった。

玉泉園庭園   P40-41
江戸初期・石川県金沢市

この地は、朝鮮京城からの捕虜として日本へ帰化した金氏が、前田家に仕え、のち脇田直賢と称して邸地を賜った所で、その子直能の代に、仙叟宗室の指導によって現在の池泉庭園が完成したという。しかし江戸中期作庭説もある。池泉は水字形といい、二か所に滝を見せる。

下時国家庭園   P42-43
江戸初期・石川県輪島市

当家は鎌倉時代の平時忠より始まるという旧家で現在書院の東南の庭と、北庭が保存されている。前者は江戸初期の様式で、後者は江戸中期と考えられる。東南庭は低い山畔を利用して枯滝と遠山石を組み、細長い池泉を掘るが、手前の苔中に打たれた飛石が味わい深い。

柴田氏庭園   P44-45
江戸初期・福井県敦賀市

当地の旧家柴田氏は、初代光有が寛文2年(1662)現地に移って屋敷を構えたのに始まる。本庭はその子清信が元禄初年に新たに邸を建て、藩主の休息所とした時代に作庭されたらしい。甘棠館という書院の南から西にかけての池泉観賞式庭園で、急な石浜の景色に特色がある。

旧玄成院庭園   P46-47
室町時代・福井県勝山市

白山神社の別当寺平泉寺の一院で、明確な歴史は明らかでないが、庭園は室町時代様式を示す。現在庭に面する書院を失っており、また池の水も失われているが、背後の自然の山畔を利用した小規模の池泉観賞式庭園で、正面上部に主木と典型的な渦巻式石組を保存している。

朝倉氏諏訪館跡庭園   P48
桃山時代・福井市

越前国の戦国大名朝倉義景によって、その本拠地一乗谷に営まれた庭園の一つ。永禄11年(1568)以降に、側室小少将局の邸に面して作庭された。上下二段の構成で、中央に巨石の滝添石を組み、その左にも山形の巨大な蓬莱石を据える。護岸石組も特に優れた造形を示す。

円照寺庭園   P49
江戸初期・福井県小浜市

もと真言宗で、文安元年(1444)現地に移され、臨済宗の寺院として再興された。本庭は池泉観賞式で、方丈の西から西南にかけて山畔を利用して作庭されている。池は小池だが、中央を出島とし、池中に岩島を配する。西南部の上方にある枯滝石組付近が特に傑出している。

龍潭寺庭園   P50
江戸初期・静岡県引佐郡

当寺は臨済禅宗の名刹で、彦根藩主井伊氏の菩提寺として名高い。本庭は本堂北庭で、現在の本堂が再建された延宝4年(1676)頃の作庭であろう。東西に長い築山を三山形式の芝山とし、その間に枯滝を作っており、下の細長い池泉には亀出島や岩島等を見せている。

摩訶耶寺庭園   P51
鎌倉時代・静岡県引佐郡

奥浜名三ケ日の地に平安時代に創立された当寺が、後山上から現地に移り、鎌倉時代中期頃に本庭が作庭されたものと推定される。池泉観賞式で、規模は大きくないが、石組には平安時代の形式を止め、蓬莱出島、鶴島石組、古式枯山水石組等、優れた造形を見せている。

妙厳寺庭園   P52-53
江戸初期・愛知県豊川市

一般に豊川稲荷の名で知られている当寺は曹洞宗の名刹で、嘉吉元年(1441)の開創。本庭は書院西庭となっている池泉観賞式庭園で、三山形式の優雅な感覚の芝山を作り、その間に枯滝を組み、手前を細長い池泉とした構成。遠江地方の特色をよく示した庭園として知られる。

地蔵院庭園   P54-55
江戸初期・三重県鈴鹿郡

関の地蔵として広く知られる真言宗御室派の寺院で、古く行基によって交通の難所鈴鹿の関に創立されたと伝える。庭園は江戸中期の作で、庫裡・書院に面し、高い山畔築山を景とする池泉観賞式庭園。池泉護岸によいものがあるが、総体的に植栽本位の庭となっている。

諸戸氏庭園   P56-57
明治時代・三重県桑名市

当地の旧家で、豪商として名高い諸戸家の庭園で、明治時代に好みにまかせて作庭された、大名好み風の池泉回遊式庭園。カキツバタを栽培し、そこに板橋の八ッ橋を架けた八ッ橋庭と、書院の池泉庭園がある。後者は旧桑名城にあった庭園の古材を用いたものといわれる。

西明寺庭園   P58-59
江戸中期・滋賀県犬上郡

平安時代承和3年(836)創立という古寺。本坊書院の南庭として残る池泉庭園は、様式上から江戸中期の作とされるが、後水害、山崩れなどのために荒廃、改造が多い。小高い築山に多数の石を組み、滝も三か所にある。池泉亀島には石橋を架ける。池泉の岩島は後補。

金剛輪寺庭園　　　　　　　　P60-61

江戸中期・末期　滋賀県愛知郡

天平時代創建という古寺。池泉庭園が三か所にあり、桃山時代作庭説もあるが誤り。現在の本坊は、安永5年(1776)に再建された明寿院で、ここに面して二庭、また少し離れて北庭がある。書院の南庭が最も豪華で、池泉に枯滝を見せ、三石の石橋を架ける。宝篋印塔も見所。

多賀神社庭園　　　　　　　　P62

桃山時代・滋賀県犬上郡

『古事記』にも記載がある古社。神仏習合時代に、不動院の庭園として作庭されたもの。当院は、豊臣秀吉が北政所の病平癒を祈願しての創立で、天正頃(1573〜91)の作。現在は社務所奥書院の庭園となっているが、一段下の地となる。石橋や、三尊石組に特色がある。

大通寺庭園　　　　　　　　　P63

江戸中期・滋賀県長浜市

当寺は真宗大谷派の長浜別院で、寛永16年(1639)の創立。寺には、旧学問所、含山軒、蘭亭の三か所に枯山水庭園が保存されており、当寺五世真央上人の時、宝暦から安永(1751〜80)にかけての作庭である。含山軒庭園は伊吹山を借景としたもの。蘭亭庭園は水墨画式の作。

普門院庭園　　　　　　　　　P64-65

江戸初期・和歌山県伊都郡

高野山の一院普門院は、元禄年中(1688〜1704)にこの地に移っており、本庭もこの頃の作庭と考えられる。庭は客殿の東庭で、東北に緑に覆われた山畔をひかえ、池泉に滝を導いている。池には大きな亀島と出島があり規模は小さいが入り組んだ変化ある地割りを見せる。

天徳院庭園　　　　　　　　　P66-67

江戸初期・和歌山県伊都郡

高野山に加賀藩主前田家によって元和8年(1622)に開かれた塔頭で、前田利常夫人の菩提を弔うための創立。天徳院は夫人の法名である。本庭は創立直後の作庭で、書院に面した池泉観賞式庭園。南部山畔には雄大な大刈込を配し、池泉には鶴亀両島を見せ、石橋を架ける。

紅葉渓庭園　　　　　　　　　P68-69

江戸初期・和歌山市

和歌山城西ノ丸御殿の庭園として築かれたもので、元和5年(1619)紀州徳川家の初祖頼宣が入城した直後に作庭にかかったもの。東は内堀を利用した広い水面とし、西は渓谷式で、南の築山に滝を落とし、地元の名石紀州青石を用いた桃山風の豪華な築山石組等が見られる。

金地院庭園　　　　　　　　　P70

江戸初期・京都市左京区

当院は南禅寺の塔頭で、黒衣の宰相といわれた崇伝の寺である。その方丈南庭は寛永6年(1629)頃より計画され、小堀遠州と庭師賢庭による作庭であった。世に「鶴亀の庭」とわれるように、鶴島・亀島・礼拝石を配した枯山水庭園で、徳川家の繁栄を祈った作庭であった。

本法寺庭園　　　　　　　　　P71

桃山時代・京都市上京区

当寺は日蓮宗で本阿弥家代々の菩提寺である。天正15年(1587)現地に移された後、慶長時代に本阿弥光悦の帰依を得、その時代に作庭されたのが方丈東の枯山水庭園である。作者は光悦であろう。奥に枯滝を組み、手前の平庭に、幡の形の蓮池と日輪の切石を配している。

瑞峰院庭園　　　　　　　　　P72

現代・京都市北区

当院は戦国大名大友宗麟の創立で、方丈は室町末期の建築である。この方丈の南・西・東に作庭された枯山水庭園は、昭和36年(1961)に現代の優れた作庭家重森三玲によって作られた。特に南の「独坐庭」は、主石に向かう石組の流れに斬新な感覚のあることで知られている。

龍源院庭園　　　　　　　　　P73

室町時代・京都市北区

名僧東渓宗牧禅師の塔頭である大徳寺山内の当院は、永正14年(1517)直後の創立という。方丈(国宝)北に作庭された「龍吟庭」は、創立当初の作と思われる平庭式枯山水庭園で、枯山水としては最古に近い。庭園正面にそそり立つ青石の石組を見せ、味わい深い空間を創造する。

城南宮庭園　　　　　　　　　P74

現代・京都市伏見区

当社は、平安時代より鳥羽離宮の地にあった城南寺の鎮守が残されたもので、方除けの神である。ここに作庭が行われたのは昭和29年(1954)で、作庭家中根金作の作。室町形式という池泉庭園と、桃山形式という枯山水庭園が中心となる。後者には豪華な石組が見られる。

勧持院庭園　　　　　　　　　P75

桃山時代・京都市下京区

移転した日蓮宗の本山本法寺の塔頭で、今も当初の地にある。当院は加藤清正によって慶長8年(1603)に再興されており、その宿坊になっていた。その頃清正によって作庭されたのが本庭であると考えられる。築山平庭結合式の枯山水で、東南部に味わい深い枯滝を見せる。

96

普門寺庭園 P76-77

江戸初期・大阪府高槻市

当寺は臨済禅宗で室町時代の創立。のち龍渓和尚によって現地に移された。後明暦元年(1655)黄檗宗に改修しているが、この頃時の作庭の名手妙蓮寺玉淵によって作庭されたのが本庭という。枯滝式枯山水の典型作で、低く枯滝や石橋を組んだ、風雅な石組が特色といえる。

安養院庭園 P78-79

桃山時代・兵庫県神戸市

天台宗の古刹太山寺の塔頭で、その歴史は不明だが、庭園は旧書院に面して作庭されたもので、現在建物は失われている。石組の豪華な造形から桃山時代の作と思われる特殊な枯山水庭園で、地元の花崗岩を使い、三か所に枯滝を組み、洞窟を設け、亀石組を遠景としている。

深田氏邸庭園 P80

伝鎌倉時代・鳥取県米子市

当地の旧家で、鎌倉時代末期に後醍醐天皇が立ち寄られたといい、本庭もその頃の作といわれるが明確ではない。旧書院に面した小規模な池泉観賞式庭園で、池中に大きく鶴島を構成し、その左に小島の亀島を作る。右手にある枯滝表現の立石三尊石組は特に力強い。

興禅寺庭園 P81

江戸初期・鳥取市

当寺は元龍峰寺といい、寛永9年(1632)岡山より移された臨済宗の寺であった。しかし萬治2年(1659)黄檗宗に改宗している。本庭はそれ以前の作で、書院北庭としての池泉観賞式庭園。広い池泉の後方に小高い築山を作り、そこに枯滝等の石組を行った風雅な庭といえる。

衆楽園庭園 P82-83

江戸初期・岡山県津山市

寛永11年(1634)津山藩主となった森長継が、明暦年間(1655～57)に津山城の北方に営んだ別邸の庭園。南北に長い広い園池を持った回遊式の大名庭園で、三島の中島を配し、橋を架けて回遊路とする。北方には滝石組や流れも保存されているが、当初の石組は少ない。

桂氏邸庭園 P84-85

江戸末期・山口県防府市

当家は毛利氏七家の内の右田毛利家の家老、桂運平忠晴に始まるという格式高い旧家である。一説に本庭は忠晴の代正徳2年(1712)の作ともいうが、これには問題がある。書院に面した特色ある枯山水庭園で、石組には横石伏石が多く、石の台に乗せた舟形石が大変珍しい。

毛利家本邸庭園 P86

明治時代・山口県防府市

有力大名であった毛利氏が、明治時代に防府に本邸を構え、ここに雄大な庭園を築造した。明治を代表する大庭園として特筆すべき存在である。起伏のある地に作庭されており、下部池泉に至る間には渓谷を思わせる数々の石組がある。大雪見燈籠の景色なども特色といえる。

万象園庭園 P87

江戸初期・香川県丸亀市

中津万象園といい、貞享5年(1688)丸亀藩主の二代京極高豊の時に、別邸として作庭された池泉回遊式の大名庭園である。京極氏は近江出身のため、園池には近江八景を取り入れたといわれる。近年改修されてはいるが、松の植栽等が豊かで、茶席「観潮楼」の景は美しい。

西江寺庭園 P88

江戸初期・愛媛県宇和島市

当寺は臨済宗で、宇和島藩初代の伊達秀宗公より的堂和尚が寛永2年(1625)寺地を賜り中興した。本庭はこの頃の作庭と思われる枯山水庭園で、書院に面して苔敷きの庭とされ、低い築山を作って枯滝を組み、中島を設け、三橋の青石橋を架けている。背景が特に豊かである。

光明寺庭園 P89

現代・福岡県太宰府市

臨済宗東福寺派に属する禅寺で、鎌倉時代の文永10年(1273)鉄牛円心和尚が渡唐天神の由来により開山。当寺の二庭は作庭家重森三玲の作で、前庭「仏光庭」は、七五三石組を光という文字に配置した作、また主庭の「一滴海庭」は、石組と白砂と苔の美しい枯山水庭園。

水前寺成趣園 P90-91

江戸初期・熊本市

熊本藩三代藩主細川綱利が、この地にあった水前寺が廃寺となった後に、寛文10年(1670)から作庭に着手した大名庭園。広大な地に当地の豊富な湧水をたたえた園池がすばらしい。東海道五十三次を意図したといい、園の中心にある富士形の築山がよき景となっている。

仙巌園(磯庭園) P92

江戸末期・鹿児島市

薩摩藩二代の島津光久が萬治年間(1658～61)に営んだ別邸の地だが、現在の景は天保年間(1830～44)に大改造されたもの。回遊式の大名庭園で「仙巌園」といい、桜島を借景として曲水をめぐらせ、モウソウチクの竹林を配するなど、中国趣味にあふれた造形が特色とされる。

Katsura Imperial Villa Garden. Early Edo period, Nishigyo-ku, Kyoto (p.10-13)

The construction of the Katsura Sanso was begin in 1620 by Tomohito Shinno of the Hachijonomiya family and completed by Tomotada, the second heir, in his reign in 1646. This very large go-round style garden is actually a large *roji* based on the teahouse garden style of the time, exhibiting the characteristic flagstone and stepping stone paths, and the stone lantern and stone wash basin.

Sentou Imperial Palace Garden. Early Edo period, Kamigyo-ku, Kyoto (p.14-17)

Construction of Gomizunoojoukou and Nyoin Gosho, to the north, began in 1627, and in the early days of construction the garden landscape artist Kobori Enshu was involved. In the middle Edo period the walls between the two premises were torn down, and the gardens combined. The dry beach of the south pond, which is comprised of stones of very even size, is called Odawara Isshouishi Beach.

Shuugakuin Imperial Villa Garden. Early Edo period, Sakyo-ku, Kyoto (p.18-21)

Construction of the detached palace for Queen Gomizunoojoukou was begun in 1656 and completed in 1659. Originally the palace was comprised of the Kamino-Ochaya (upper teahouse) and Shimono-Ochaya (lower teahouse), the former being Rinuntei, which has a splendid view of the very large pond. What is now referred to as the Nakano-Ochaya (middle teahouse) was originally the old Rinkyu-ji temple, which was joined to the palace grounds in the Meiji period.

Gyokusen-ji Temple Garden. Early Edo period, Higashitagawa-gun, Yamagata Prefecture (p.22)

Gyokusenji, the old Soto sect temple in Haguro-machi, is said to have been built in the middle Kamakura period. The garden, a viewing-style pond garden, is situated on the north side of the temple. There is a low mound upon which a rock waterfall sits, and three islands in the pond. The stepping stones in the foreground were added in the Meiji period, it is believed. The formation of the rocks is superb; unfortunately, the view is obscured by the shrubbery.

Shiramizu Amida-do Garden. Heian period, Iwaki, Fukushima Prefecture (p.23)

Ganjo-ji's pond garden was built in the Jodo garden-style of the late Heian period. Founded in 1160 by Iwaki Norimichi, this temple's rooms were used by Fujiwara Hidehira's sister, Tokuhime. The pond and garden were recently excavated and restored, with the Amida-do to the north as the centerpiece. A superb example of the feeling of the period is the rock island in the east pond.

Kairakuen Garden. Late Edo period, Mito, Ibaragi Prefecture (p.24-25)

Originally a plum orchard belonging to Tokugawa Nariakira, the ninth son of the Mito clan of the Tokugawa family, it was turned into a garden to be enjoyed together with the public in 1840; thus the name, Kairakuen. The two-storied *Kobuntei* stands at its center, and the view of Lake Chinami is still an important feature. In the Meiji era the garden's name was changed to Tokiwa Public Garden.

Rinno-ji Temple Shouyouen Garden. Late Edo period, Nikko, Tochigi Prefecture (p.26-27)

The garden of Rinnoji, the Tendai Sect temple in Toushouguu, is thought to have been built just after 1648. It is a large garden with a view of Mt. Nantai and a long go-round pond that stretches from east to west. There has been some restoration, but much of the original garden remains, including the rock formation of the rock island, and the prized five-tiered stone lantern, which is from the early Edo period.

Kiyozumien Garden. Meiji period, Koto-ku, Tokyo (p.28-31)

This garden was built by Iwasaki Yataro, founder of the Mitsui zaibatsu, on the ruins of the famous Edo period garden belonging to Kuze Yamatonokami. Construction was started in 1878 and completed in 1891. At the time it borrowed water form the Sumida River. There are various islands in the pond, all of them built with stones from the great rockeries of the country.

East garden of the Imperial Palace. Early Edo period, Chiyoda-ku, Tokyo (p.32-33)

Records state that construction of the Gyoen Teien, which faces Ninomaru Palace of the old Edo castle, began in 1630, and that it was rebuilt in 1645. There have been many restorations since, and the go-round style garden offers many splendid views, including a beautiful rock waterfall at its center, a rock beach, and a snow-viewing stone lantern.

Former Shiba Imperial Villa Garden. Early Edo period, Minato-ku, Tokyo (p.34-35)

The lord of Shimofusa-sakura (present day Chiba Prefecture), Oukubo Tadatomo, built this garden in 1678, when it was named Rakujuen. In 1696 additions were made on the east side and the temple took on its present form. This is the representative example of an ocean-inlet-style garden, very large and containing many islands. The dyke is a Chinese-style *seiko zutsumi*.

Sankeien Garden. Taisho era, Yokohama, Kanagawa Prefecture (p.36-37)

Construction on this mountain retreat of zaibatsu leader Hara Tomitaro was begun in 1899 and completed in 1908. It is a go-round style garden, with inner and outer premises now separated. The inner garden is very rich in old architecture and fine stone craft works collected from around the country. The area around the Rinshunkaku pavilion is particularly rich in fine settings.

Shimizuen Garden. Early Edo period, Shibata, Niigata Prefecture (p.38-39)

Nobunao, the third generation Mizoguchi leader of the Shibata clan, built his castle residence (*shimoyashiki*) in 1665, and had its garden designed by the Enshu sect tea ceremony master Agata Sochi. This famous large pond garden of the go-round-style has temples and tea drinking seats placed all about. Recent restorations have rendered it very beautiful.

Gyokusenen Garden. Early Edo period, Kanazawa, Ishikawa Prefecture (p.40-41)

Kim-shi, a prisoner taken from the capital palace of Korea and brought to Japan to live with the Maeda family, later changed his name to Wakita Naokata. According to records he had a son, Naonobu, who under the direction of the Senso Soshitsu religous sect built the pond garden which appears today. But there is the possibility this garden was built in the middle Edo period. The pond has two waterfalls and takes the shape of the Chinese ideograph for water.

Shimotokikuni Family Garden. Early Edo period, Wajima, Ishikawa Prefecture (p.42-43)

This residence is a very old one established by Taira Tokitada in the Kamakura period. The drawing room now has a southeast garden and north garden. It is thought that the former was built in the style of the early Edo period, the latter in the middle Edo period. The southeast garden has a low mound and dry waterfall (*karetaki*) and *enzan* (distant mountain) rock formation. The stepping stones in the foreground along the narrow pond are particularly nice.

Shibata Residence Garden. Early Edo period, Tsuruga, Fukui Prefecture (p.44-45)

Mitsuari, first son of the old Shibata family, moved to this location in 1662 and built his residence. His son, Kiyonobu, added his own residence and this garden for the pleasure of the head of the clan. The pond-viewing garden stretches from the south to the west side of the Kantokan, as the drawing room is called. It is noteworthy for its steep rock beaches.

Former Genjo-in Temple Garden. Muromachi period, Katsuyama, Fukui Prefecture (p.46-47)

Genjoin is one of the buildings of Heisen-ji Temple, which belongs to Hakusan-jinja Shrine, but outside the fact that its garden is in the Muromachi style, its history is not clearly known. The buildings that once fronted the garden have been lost, and the pond too is dry, but the small-scale pond-viewing style garden is still evident from the main trees in the center and the classic whirlpool-style rock formation.

Asakura Suwayakata Residence Garden Ruins. Momoyama period, Fukui (p.48)

This garden was one of several owned by Asakura Yoshikage, the powerful Echizen daimyo of the Sengoku period, in his home base location of Ichijoudani. It was built after 1568 at the residence of his mistress, Shoushounotsubone. It has an upper and lower level, and a huge central rock in a "rock and waterfall" style formation. To the left is another very large "lotus leaf" style rock. The waterbreak rock formation is also considered a fine example of its kind.

Enshou-ji Temple Garden. Early Edo period, Obama, Fukui Prefecture (p.49)

Originally, in 1444, the Shingon sect established a temple here, and this was later restored by the Rinzai sect. The main garden is a viewing garden built around a mound extending from west to southwest. The pond is small but contains a *dejima* and central rock formation. The *karetaki* rock formation above the southwest end is considered particularly brilliant work.

Ryutan-ji Temple Garden. Early Edo period, Inasa-gun, Shizuoka Prefecture (p.50)

At the time this was an old Rinzai sect temple famous as the burial place of the Hikone clan lords. The garden belongs to the main building of the temple, and was constructed when it was rebuilt, in 1676. The mountain formation is of the *sanzon* (three mountain), grass-covered style, and stretches from east to west, with a *karetaki* in the middle, with turtle and rock islands in the narrow pond below.

Makaya-ji Temple Garden. Kamakura period, Inasa-gun, Shizuoka Prefecture (p.51)

It is believed that this temple was first established in the Heian period, on higher ground to the rear, but was moved to its present location and rebuilt during the middle Kamakura period, when the main garden was built. The garden is of the pond-viewing style, and not large, but the style is perfectly Heian, with a *horai* style peninsula, crane island, old style dry rock formation (*koshiki karesansui*) and other excellent formations.

Myougon-ji Temple Garden. Early Edo period, Toyokawa, Aichi Prefecture (p.52-53)

Famous as the temple of Toyokawa Inari, this old Soto Sect temple was founded in 1441. The main garden is a pond-viewing garden on the west side of the temple, which consist of a beautiful three mountain grass-covered formation with a *karetaki* and narrow pond. The garden is a famous example of the Tootoumi region's style.

Jizou-in Temple Garden. Early Edo period, Suzuka-gun, Mie Prefecture (p.54-55)

Widely known for the *sekinojizo* (Stone Buddhas of the Barrier), this Shingon Omuro sect temple was erected by this monk Gyouki. The garden was built in the middle Edo period and fronts the storage room (*kuri*) and temple. The viewing-style pond garden has a high artifical mound (*sampan*), and there is a waterbreak formation in the pond. For the most part this garden is notable for its shrubbery.

Moroto Family Garden. Meiji era, Kuwana, Mie Prefecture (p.56-57)

The gardens of this renowned merchant family were constructed around the family estate in the popular styles of the Meiji era. They include the very popular go-round style pond-garden, a garden of rabbit-ear irises, a *yatsuhashi* (eight-bridge) garden, and a garden off the drawing room. The latter was reportedly constructed of materials removed from the old Kuwana Castle garden.

Saimyo-ji Temple Garden. Middle Edo period, Inukami-gun, Shiga Prefecture (p.58-59)

This ancient temple is said to have been built in the third year of Showa (836), during the Heian period. The remaining garden is situated to the south of the main drawing room, and is said to be from the middle Edo period, although as a result of flooding and landslides it was abandoned and rebuilt many times. Many stones are assembled among hillocks of various heights, and there are three waterfalls. A stone bridge leads to the *kamejima* (turtle island.) The rock island is a later addition.

Kongorin-ji Temple Garden. Middle-late Edo period, Echi-gun, Shiga Prefecture (p.60-61)

This ancient temple is said to have been built in the Tempei period. There are three pond gardens, mistakenly reported to have been built in the Momoyama period. In fact, the main drawing room which exists today was rebuilt in 1776 as the Myoju-in. Two gardens are built beside it, and a third, the North Garden, is some distance away. The garden on the south side of the drawing room is the most resplendent, exhibiting a *karetaki* in the pond, a three-stone bridge and a *houkyouintou* style monument.

Tentoku-in Temple Garden. Early Edo period, Ito-gun, Wakayama Prefecture (p.66-67)

The head of the Maeda family, which lead the Kaga clan of Kouyasan, built this temple in 1622 to honor the soul of his wife, Toshitsune. Tentoku-in utilizes the wife's posthumous Buddhist name. The main garden was built soon after the temple was opened. Set beside the drawing room, it is a *kansho* (viewing) style pond garden, with a large and deeply-cut southern hillock and pond with a stork island, turtle island and stone bridge.

Zuiho-in Temple Garden. Modern, Kita-ku, Kyoto (p.72)

This temple was built by the Sengoku period daimyo Ootomo Sorin, and the *hojo* itself is from the Muromachi period. The *karesansui* that now surrounds the south, west and east sides of the *hojo* was built in 1961 and is the work of the expert garden artist Shigemori Mirei. The line of rocks that leads toward the big stone in the Dokuzatei garden is noted for its powerful feeling.

Taga-jinja Shrine Garden. Middle Edo period, Inukami-gun, Shiga Prefecture (p.62)

This ancient shrine is mentioned in the *kojiki* (Records of Ancient Matters). Built during a time when both Buddhism and Shintoism flourished, it contains a temple and garden. The garden was erected by Toyotomi Hideyoshi as an offering for the recovery of his wife from illness, and dates from Tensei (1573-91). It is a part of the Shrine's main office drawing room, although set at a lower level. It is characterized by a stone bridge and sanzon stone arrangements.

Momiji-dani Garden. Early Edo period, Wakayama (p.68-69)

Built immediately after the first descendent of the Kishu Tokugawa family, Yorinobu, took control of Wakayama castle, in 1619, the garden was originally known as the Nishinomaru garden. The eastern side utilizes the inner moat as a large expanse of water, the western side exhibits the ravine style, and the south shows an artificial mountain and waterfall. Momoyama-style "mountains" and other stone assemblies of beautiful Kishu bluestone are among the attractions.

Ryogen-in Temple Garden. Muromachi period, Kita-ku, Kyoto (p.73)

The temple of the noted Tokei Souboku, Ryogen-in was built just after 1517. The *hojo* is a national treaure, and the flat *karesansui*-style garden on the north side is thought to date from the time of the temple's construction, placing it among the oldest examples in existence. The bluerock stone formation at the front of the garden helps to create a space of unique depth.

Daitsu-ji Temple Garden. Middle Edo period, Nagahama, Shiga Prefecture (p.63)

The temple was originally erected in 1639 as the Nagahama temple of the Shinsu Outani sect. The temple is comprised of the old academy, the Ganzan and the Rantei, each of which overlooks a *karesansui* garden. The gardens were built during the tenure of the temple's fifth priest, Shino Shonin, between 1751-1780. The Ganzan garden employs Mt.Ibuki as a backdrop. The Rantei garden is in the india ink painting style.

Konchi-in Temple Garden. Early Edo period, Sakyo-ku, Kyoto (p.70)

This temple was the main pillar of the Nanzen-ji Temple, and the one which practiced the so-called "priest of black clothes" faith. Its southern garden was planned around 1629 and built by Kobori Enshu and Kentei. It is called the Crane and Turtle Garden in the profession, and was built to honour the Tokugawas. It has crane and turtle rock formations, and a worshipping stone.

Jonangu Garden. Modern, Fushimi-ku, Kyoto (p.74)

The Hoyoke Shrine (for protection from evil spirits) was part of JonanTemple, which was connected to Toba Detached Palace, which dated from the Heian period. The garden was built in 1954, and is the work of Nakane Kinsaku. A pond garden in the Muromachi style, and a *karesansui* in the Momoyama style, are the central elements. The latter exhibits a fine rock formation.

Fumon-in Temple Garden. Early Edo period, Ito-gun, Wakayama Prefecture (p.64-65)

One of the temples of Kouyasan, Fumon-in moved to this area during Genroku (1688-1704) era, at which time the present garden is thought to have been built. The garden is situated to the east of the guest room, and utilizes a leafy sampan at its northeast side to provide a waterfall for the pond. The pond is small but noteworthy for its large *kamejima* and *dejima*, and numerous other variations.

Hompou-ji Temple Garden. Momoyama period, Kamigyo-ku, Kyoto (p.71)

This temple harbors the remains of the generations of the Honami family. In 1587 it was moved to this place and later, when Honami Koetsu took the vows of the temple, the *karesansui* style garden to the east of the priest's living quarters (*hojo*) was built. The designer was probably Koetsu himself. In the background is a dry waterfall, in the foreground a Buddhist *ban* and stone sun wheel.

Kanji-in Temple Garden. Momoyama period, Shimogyo-ku, Kyoto (p.75)

The headquarters of the Nichiren Sect was moved to this location and remains here to this day. The temple was restored by Katoh Kyomasa, and it is believed that he built the garden as well. It is a *karesansui* using a mixture of artificial mountain and flat garden styles, and has a particularly elegant dry waterfall (*karetaki*) at the southeast end.

Fumon-ji Temple Garden. Early Edo period, Takatsuki, Osaka (p.76-77)

This temple was established by the Rinzai sect in the Muromachi period. Later it was moved by the head monk Ryukei to its present location. Later still it was restored by Oobakushu, and at this time the garden was built by the famous garden artist Myorenji Gyokuen. It is a classic example of a *kareike-karesansui* garden, and has a low dry rock waterfall and stone bridge. The rock formation is quite unique.

Jurakuen Garden. Early Edo period, Tsuyama, Okayama Prefecture (p.82-83)

Built as a second residence on the north side of Tsuyama castle by Mouri Nagatsugu, who became head of the Tsuyama clan in 1634, this wide go-round-style garden stretches from north to south and includes a three island formation, as well as a hanging bridge for the go-round path. There is a rock waterfall at the north end which continues to flow, but few of the original rocks remain.

Seigou-ji Temple Garden. Early Edo period, Uwajima, Ehime Prefecture (p.88)

The land under this Rinzai Sect temple was presented to the priest Tekido by Date Hidemune, who was the first clan leader of Uwajima. This *karesansui* style garden is thought to have been built at the same time. It includes an expanse of grass before the temple, a low mountain formation and drywaterfall, a central island and three bridges made of bluestone. It is a garden of very rich scenery.

Anyo-in Temple Garden. Momoyama period, Kobe, Hyogo Prefecture (p.78-79)

This is the leading tower of the Tendai Sect's Taizan-ji Temple. Its history is unknown, but the garden is known to have fronted a temple building which has been lost. Because of the lovely formation of the rocks it is suspected that this uniqu *karesansui* garden dates from the Momoyama period. It employs the local granite, and has dry rock waterfalls in three places, a cave and a turtle island.

Katsura Residence Garden. Late Edo period, Bofu, Yamaguchi Prefecture (p.84-85)

This residence was established by Katsura Umpei Tadaharu, who was the righthand man of Migita Mouri, leader of one of the seven Mouri families. One explanationhas it that the garden is the work of Tadaharu, but there is a problem with this theory. The rock formation in this *karesansui* contains many flat and vertical rocks, as well as a very rare "boat" rock on a pedestal.

Koumyou-ji Temple Garden. Modern, Dazaifu, Fukuoka Prefecture (p.89)

This temple is under the administration of the Toufuku-ji Sect of the Rinzai faith, and was originally opened in 1273 by the priest Tetsugyu Enshin at the place where the God Totoutenjin was said to depart for China. The two gardens were created by the garden architect Shigemori Mirei. The former, the Bukko Garden, contains rock formations composed of 7, 5 and 3 rocks and resembles the Chinese character for "light". The main garden is a lovely *karesansui* known as the *itteki-kaitei* (one-drop ocean garden), which is comprised of a very beautiful rock formation, sand and moss.

Fukada Residence Garden. Kamakura period, Yonago, Tottori Prefecture (p.80)

It is said that Emperor Godaigo once stopped at this old family residence, and that the garden was built at this time. This small pond-viewing garden is situated were the old temple once was, and contains a large crane island and, to the left, a smaller turtle island. It also has a dry waterfall showing a very strong *sanzon* rock formation.

Mouri Central Residence Garden. Meiji era, Bofu, Yamaguchi Prefecture (p.86)

The powerful daimyo Mouri built his home residence in Bofu in the Meiji era. It included a very large garden, one which is representative of the works of the era. The natural undulations of the land have been utilized, with the many rock formations leading down to the lower pond suggesting a natural ravine. The snow viewing stone lantern is also a rarity.

Suizen-ji Joushuen Garden. Early Edo period, Kumamoto (p.90-91)

This famous garden was built in 1670 by Hosokawa Tsunatoshi, the thirdlord of the Kumamoto clan, on the ruins of the old Suizenji Temple. The garden's large pond is fed by natural springs and is a truly wonderful sight. The garden was intended to represent the next station after the 53rd station of the Tokai Highway; thus the central mound in the garden was made to resemble Mt. Fuji.

Kouzen-ji Temple Garden. Early Edo period, Tottori (p.81)

This temple was formerly Ryuhou-ji. It is a Rinzai Sect temple which was moved from Okayama in 1632. In 1659 Oobakushu restored it, but the garden dates from earlier times, being of the pond-viewing variety and built on the north side of the temple. Behind the pond is a fairly high mountain rock formation with a dry waterfall and other elements. In all it is a finely balanced garden.

Banshoen Garden. Early Edo period, Marugame, Kagawa Prefecture (p.87)

Called Nakatsu Banshoen, this go-round-style garden was constructed as part of a second residence by second generation clan leader Kyogoku Takatoyo. Since Kyogoku was from Oumi, he wanted the garden to contain the chief sights of Oumi. The garden has been much restored in recent years, and is noteworthy for its rich planted pines and the beautiful scenery of its "kanchoro" teahouse.

Senganen (Iso) Garden. Late Edo period, Kagoshima (p.92)

The garden is built on the grounds of the villa of the second lord of the Satsuma clan, Shimazu Mitsuhisa (1658-61), but was in fact greatly restored between 1830-44. This large go-round style garden is also referred to as "Senganen". With Mt. Sakurajima as its background the garden uses winding waterways and various bamboo groves, creating effects like those seen in Chinese gardens.

「庭園様式について」

吉河　功

■日本庭園の大分類

　大きな視点から分類した場合，日本庭園は次の三つの種類に分けることができる。

　　　　池泉庭園
　　　　枯山水庭園
　　　　茶庭 (露地)

　ここでは，この三種について簡単に解説を加え，さらに次の項ではその様式をやや詳しく見て行くことにしたい。

池泉庭園

　池を掘り，そこに水をたたえた庭園で，日本庭園が発祥した飛鳥・奈良時代以降，今日まで連綿として作り続けられている。古くから位の高い人々によって作られた大規模な池泉は，園池といい，池中に島々を配置し，実際に舟を浮かべて楽しんだものであった。その基本には蓬萊神仙の別世界に遊ぶという，中国からもたらされた思想があり，この発想は長く日本庭園の伝統となって，庭作りに大きな影響を与えている。

枯山水庭園

　室町時代の中期に，京都で応仁の乱が勃発し，都はその大半を焼失した。

　その復興の過程で成立してきたのが，水を一切使わない庭園形式である枯山水庭園であった。したがってその成立は室町時代後期であり，京の名高い禅寺である大徳寺，妙心寺の，いずれかの寺院から発祥したものと考えられる。

　白砂を敷いて水景を象徴する庭園は，精神性の高い造形として，日本庭園の大きな特色となった。

茶庭 (露地)

　室町時代末期から，桃山時代初期にかけて，茶の湯というものが成立すると，その茶会を行うために必要な設備として，それまでには無かった，まったく新しい考え方の実用の庭が作られるようになる。それは茶室に入るまでの通路であり，したがって古くは「路地」の文字が使われたものである。

　ここには，茶会に必要な様々な設備が配されたから，観賞が主体の庭園とはまったく異なったものとなった。通路を主体とするから，この茶庭の出現によって，初めて敷石・飛石・手水鉢・石燈籠などが導入されたのである。

■庭園様式の分類

　以上に述べた，池泉庭園，枯山水庭園，茶庭 (露地) には，さらに色々な形式があり，それを一般に庭園様式と呼んでいる。

　それを詳しく紹介するだけの紙面はないが，ここではその概略だけを記しておくことにするので，庭園観賞の参考にして頂ければ幸いである。

　池泉庭園には，次の四種が考えられる。

池泉庭園 ─┬─ ① 池泉舟遊式庭園
　　　　　├─ ② 池泉回遊式庭園
　　　　　├─ ③ 池泉観賞式庭園
　　　　　└─ ④ 流水観賞式庭園

①池泉舟遊式庭園は，園池に舟を浮かべて楽しむものであるが，それと共に建物からもその景色を眺めた。舟はそこに乗って舟遊びをする目的と，舟に楽人を乗せて，音楽を奏でながら舟遊させることもかなり行われた。

②池泉回遊式庭園は，池泉の周囲に曲がりくねった道を通し，そこを歩きながら変化ある景色を楽しむことが主体となった庭園である。江戸時代の大名庭園は，多くがこの様式とされていた。

③池泉観賞式庭園は，日本庭園の中では最も例の多いもので，書院の発達によって，建物内から見ることが主目的となっている庭園である。どちらかといえば，庭園は①②より小規模なものとなる。こういう観賞式庭園でもその一部には道が作られるのが普通だが，それは手入れ等の便宜のための道で，そこからの観賞が主体ではない。しかし道があれば回遊式だと誤解している人が多いので，注意してほしい。

④流水観賞式庭園は，池泉ではなく，庭園内に流れを作って，それを中心に観賞するものである。水の豊富な地方でないと作庭できないので，実例はかなり少ない。

枯山水庭園は，ほとんどが小規模の庭園であり，建物からの観賞主体の庭であるから，また別の角度から分類される。

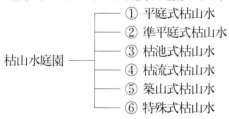

枯山水庭園 ─┬─ ① 平庭式枯山水
　　　　　　├─ ② 準平庭式枯山水
　　　　　　├─ ③ 枯池式枯山水
　　　　　　├─ ④ 枯流式枯山水
　　　　　　├─ ⑤ 築山式枯山水
　　　　　　└─ ⑥ 特殊式枯山水

①平庭式枯山水は，全体が平面となった地に作られるもので，龍安寺庭園（室町・京都市）に代表されるようなもの。

②準平庭式枯山水は，平庭の一部に低い土盛りを作って，枯滝等を表現した枯山水。

③枯池式枯山水は，中心部に枯池を設けたもので，それにも象徴式枯池と，池泉式枯池とがある。

④枯流式枯山水は，全体に枯流れを作ったもので，高低差のある土地にふさわしい枯山水。大仙院庭園（室町・京都市）等はその典型である。

⑤築山式枯山水は，築山を主体としたもので，下の部分は平庭としたり，枯池としたりする。全国的にかなり実例も多い。

⑥特殊式枯山水は，以上のいずれにも該当しない特殊な形式のものをいう。

茶庭（露地）はその目的が，他の庭園とはまったく異なるから，分類もまた別の角度からということになる。

茶庭(露地) ─┬─ ① 草庵式露地
　　　　　　└─ ② 書院式露地

①草庵式露地は，茶室が草庵であり庭内に独立して設けられたり，書院の一部に付属したりする。佗好みが主体とされるから，山道のような風情が好まれる。

②書院式露地は，武家の茶の系統で，書院庭園に近い感覚を持っているが，飛石や手水鉢は必ず用いられる。

また，茶庭は古い時代は一重露地であったが，その後に中門を設けた二重露地，三重露地が作られるようになった。したがって，

茶庭(露地) ─┬─ ① 一重露地
　　　　　　├─ ② 二重露地
　　　　　　└─ ③ 三重露地

という分類も行われている。この他にも，日本庭園は多方面からの分類が可能であり，それらを総合的に見ていく必要があるが，ここではその内の最も基本的なものだけを紹介した。

103

The Styles of Japanese Gardens   Isao Yoshikawa

A General Classification

Broadly speaking, one can separate Japanese gardens into three categories:

    Gardens with ponds (*chisen teien*)

    Dry rock gardens (*karesansui teien*)

    Teahouse gardens (*chaniwa, roji*)

    Here I would like to briefly explain each of the three types. Later I will discuss their characteristics in further detail.

Gardens with Ponds (*chisen teien*)

    Gardens with artificial ponds have been built in Japan since the Asuka and Nara periods, and continue to be constructed to this day. Very large gardens with ponds, referred to as "pond gardens", have been built by people of high rank since ancient times. In olden days many of the ponds had island and were large enough for people to float boats upon for recreation. Behind the development of this landscape was the Chinese legend of *horaishinsen*, or the "other world," which has profoundly influenced the design of the Japanese garden.

Dry rock gardens (*karesansui teien*)

    During the middle of the Muromachi period the Onin Wars took place, and over half of Kyoto was burned. During the resurrection of the city the *karesansui* garden style, or dry rock garden, was developed. Therefore the style was begun in Kyoto, during the latter half of the Muromachi period. The original examples are thought to have been created at the famous Kyoto temples Daitoku-ji and Myoshin-ji. The sea of white sand, with its highly spiritual connotations, has become one of the unique characteristics of the Japanese rock garden.

Teahouse gardens (*chaniwa, roji*)

    Between the end of the Muromachi period and the beginning of the of the Momoyama period the tea ceremony developed and came into wide practice, and as one of its props a specific style of garden was developed. The main element in it was the path leading to the teahouse. Originally, this path was referred to as the *roji*. The *roji* can consist of flag or stepping stones, and along its way two other key elements of the teahouse garden are found, the stone water basin (*chozubachi*) and stone lantern (*ishidourou*).

A Further Classification of Garden Styles

    Beyond the three basic kinds of garden - gardens with ponds, gardens without actual water (dry rock gardens) and teahouse gardens - one can make many further distinctions in type. Let us call these the garden *styles*.

    There is not space enough here to introduce all the variations, but a summary can be offered which will hopefully benefit viewers of gardens.

Among gardens with ponds (*chisen teien*) are the following styles:

Gardens with ponds (*chisen teien*):

    1. Boating style pond gardens (*chisen shuuyuushiki teien*)

    2. Go-round style pond gardens (*chisen kaiyuushiki teien*)

    3. Pond-viewing style gardens (*chisen kanshoshiki teien*)

    4. Flowing water style gardens (*ryusui kanshoushiki teien*)

1) As the name suggests, boating style ponds were built for people to enjoy from boats, but they were also designed to be viewed from nearby buildings. Besides floating on the pond for pleasure, musicians were often made to play on boats for guests seated in the garden.

2) Go-round style gardens had a path completely around the pond so that people could stroll around the pond and enjoy all the views. Many of the great

gardens of the Edo period were of this kind.

3) Pond-viewing gardens are the most common kind of pond garden in Japan, and developed along with the temples themselves, from which they can always be viewed. In size these tend to be smaller gardens than either 1 or 2. Viewing gardens also have paths, but the paths are more utilitarian, and do not always afford a view. People often mistakenly assume that any path in a garden will be of the circular type, but this is not always the case.

4) Flowing water gardens utilize flowing water, rather than a pond, as the main object of viewing. Because these gardens can only be built in areas with a wealth of flowing water they are relatively rare.

Dry rock gardens (*karesansui teien*):

    1. Flat dry rock style gardens (*hiraniwaskiki karesansui*)

    2. Flat dry rock style gardens with hillocks (*jun hiraniwashiki karesansui*)

    3. Dry pond style dry rock gardens (*kareikeshiki karesansui*)

    4. Dry stream style dry rock gardens (*karenagareshiki karesansui*)

    5. Mountain style dry rock gardens (*tsukiyamashiki karesansui*)

    6. Special style dry rock gardens (*tokushushiki karesansui*)

1) Flat dry rock gardens are gardens which are built on flat ground. One of the representative examples is Ryoan-ji (Muromachi period, Kyoto).

2) Flat dry rock gardens sometimes contain a low raised area where one finds a dry waterfall (*karetaki*) or other elements.

3) Dry pond rock gardens contain a symbolic pond at their center. There are also *shouchoushiki karesansui* (symbolic dry pond gardens) and *chisenshiki karesansui* (pond style dry rock gardens).

4) Dry stream style rock gardens are built where the land naturally slopes, and is therefore suited to a stream. A classic example is Daisen-in garden (Muromachi period, Kyoto).

5) The mountain style rock garden is usually built over a flat garden or dry pond formation. There are quite a few examples of this type of garden in Japan.

6) Special style dry rock gardens are any which do not fall into one of the above categories.

    Teahouse (*chaniwa, roji*) gardens serve a very different purpose from the gardens discussed above, and their manner of classification is thus different.

Teahouse gardens(*Chaniwa, roji*):

    1. Thatch-roof teahouse gardens (*souanshiki roji*)

    2. Temple teahouse gardens (*shoin shiki roji*)

1) The thatch-roof teahouse garden has a thatched arbor as its centerpiece, but is also attached to a temple. Normally these gardens have scenery like that of amountain road, to promote the sense of isolation.

2) Temple teahouse gardens are like the tea gardens found in the homes of samurai. At temple teahouse gardens one always finds a stepping stone path (*tobiishi*) and stone water basin (*chozubachi*).

    Moreover, while teahouse gardens were originally one-level gardens, they were later created in two and three-level garden styles. Therefore, one can make the following further classification:

Teahouse gardens (*chaniwa, roji*):

    1. One-level gardens (*ichiju roji*)

    2. Two-level gardens (*niju roji*)

    3. Three-level gardens (*sanju roji*)

    The classification of Japanese gardens can surely be approached from other directions, and it is useful to study other approaches, but for the purpose of an introduction to the subject these basic distinctions are the most useful.

協力者一覧

朝倉氏遺跡調査研究所
安養院
NHK 出版
円照寺
㈱島津興業
偕楽園
観持院
桂氏
玉川寺
清澄庭園
旧芝離宮管理事務所
玉泉園
宮内庁京都事務所
金剛輪寺
興禅寺
光明寺
三渓園
西明寺
西江寺
清水園
下時国家
柴田氏甘棠館
地蔵院
城南宮
衆楽園
水前寺成趣園
仙巌園
多賀大社
大通寺
大徳寺瑞峰院
大徳寺龍源院
天徳院
南禅寺金地院
万象園
平泉寺
普門院
普門寺
深田氏邸
本法寺
摩訶耶寺
妙巌寺
毛利氏本邸
諸戸精文
龍潭寺
輪王寺逍遥園
和歌山紅葉渓庭園

(敬称略　五十音順)

あとがき
Postscript

庭園は，全国に約1000以上あるといわれています。日本各地には，その土地の名石や植栽を使った特色ある庭園が多く造られました。

庭には，平等院・浄瑠璃寺などの浄土世界を表現した庭，龍安寺・大徳寺方丈など禅の思想の庭，水前寺成趣園のような自然風景を取り入れた庭など，さまざまな庭があり，見る者の心をなごませてくれます。この写真集には，青森から鹿児島に至る各地の庭を収めましたが，少しでも郷土のことを思い出してなつかしんでいただければ幸いです。

最後に，出版にあたり，こころよく写真撮影・掲載を御許可くださいました方々に心よりお礼申し上げます。また，今回も玉稿を贈ってくださった吉河功先生はじめ，ブックデザインの奥山有美さんやグラフィック社の岡本義正氏にも厚くお礼を申し上げます。

日弁 貞夫

106

It is said that there are over 1,000 *teien* gardens in Japan. Many of these gardens are designed with local stones and shrubbery, and express the unique qualities of their region.

Among the gardens of Japan are those of the Joudo world, such as Byoudou-in and Joururi-ji, and those of the Zen school of thought, such as Ryouan-ji and Daitoku-ji's *houjou*, and still others which utilize the scenery of the natural world, like Suizenji Joshuen. These various kinds of gardens all have the effect of calming the mind of the viewer. This collection of gardens covers regions ranging from Aomori to Kagoshima, and it is one of the hopes of the author that these plates will remind some readers of their home country.

Finally, in respect to the publication of this book, I would like to express heartfelt thanks the photographers who gave us permission to use their pictures. Special thanks are also due to Mr. Isao Yoshikawa, who contributed his excellent commentary, as well as to graphic designer Miss. Yumi Okuyama and Graphic-sha's Mr. Yoshimasa Okamoto.

Sadao Hibi

日弉貞夫　<small>ひびさだお</small>　略歴

1947年　大阪に生まれる。
　　　　日本写真専門学校卒業。
　　　　スタジオ・フラッシュ勤務を経て
　　　　フリーランスとなり，現在に至る。
　　　　日本写真家協会会員。

著書
1975年　『写真集丹後路』(講談社)。『小京都撮影ガイド』(朝日ソノラマ)
1977年　『日本の庭』(朝日ソノラマ)。『斑鳩の道』(駸々堂出版)
1978年　『心──日本〈英文版〉』(和伸社)。『日本の城』(朝日ソノラマ)
1979年　『丹後・若狭路』(保育社)
1980年　『熊野路の魅力』(淡交社)。『戦国合戦絵屛風集成』
　　　　(中央公論社)。『大和・熊野路の音』(日本写真企画)
1981年　『カメラ風土記・兵庫』(保育社)
1983年　『大坂冬の陣・夏の陣』(PHP研究所)。『関ケ原合戦』
　　　　(PHP研究所)。『陶工・富本憲吉の世界』(文化出版局)
　　　　『女人書譜』(駸々堂出版)。『戦国合戦図』(保育社)
　　　　『若狭の道』(旺文社)
1985年　『古田織部の書状』(毎日新聞社)。『日本美術に描かれた女性
　　　　たち』(朝日新聞社)
1986年　『四季法隆寺』(新潮社)。『高麗・李朝の螺鈿』(毎日新聞社)
　　　　『日本の名庭』(朝日新聞社)
1987年　『日本の伝統・色とかたち』〈衣・食・住〉全3巻(グラフィック社)
1989年　『小京都物語』(グラフィック社)。『灰皿』(現代企画室)
　　　　『JAPANESE DETAIL』全3巻(Chronicle books)
1990年　『日本の伝統文様』全2巻(グラフィック社)。『江戸のサイエ
　　　　ンス図鑑』(インテグラ)。『井伊家の名宝』(毎日新聞社)
1992年　『日本の伝統・色とかたち』〈遊芸〉(グラフィック社)
1993年　『歌舞伎衣裳』(講談社)。『日本の名勝庭園』(グラフィック社)

使用カメラ　：リンホフテヒニカ，トヨフィールド，アサヒペンタックス6×7
使用レンズ　：4×5判-90ミリ・105ミリ・135ミリ・150ミリ・180ミリ・210ミリ・240ミリ・300ミリ・360ミリ・450ミリ・600
　　　　　　ミリ，6×7判―55ミリ・75ミリ・105ミリ・150ミリ・200ミリ・300ミリ

事務所　(株) フォトアトリエSADANORI
　　　　〒150 東京都渋谷区神南1丁目13の12 神南ハウス2F
　　　　電話 (03)3462-2877

ふるさとの名庭　日氐貞夫写真集

A CELEBRATION OF JAPANESE GARDENS
Photographs by SADAO HIBI

1994年3月25日　初版第1刷発行

著　者●日氐貞夫 ⓒ
発行者●久世利郎
印刷所●日本写真印刷株式会社
製本所●日本写真印刷株式会社
写　植●三和写真工芸株式会社
発行所●株式会社グラフィック社
　　　〒102 東京都千代田区九段北1-9-12
　　　電話 03-3263-4318　FAX 03-3263-5279
　　　落丁・乱丁はお取替えいたします。
ISBN4-7661-0744-6 ⓒ 0072